Are You Home?

Isabella Fulbright

To my parents. Thank you for everything.

Contents

Prologue

Origination

I grew up in a small town in Florida, the type with a main street and train tracks, a local waffle house and a Dunkin' Donuts. I was a toddler when we moved there. It's where I spent my childhood.

At the age of two, I could walk. I spent my time outside with my two older sisters, my parents, our animals.

At the age of four, I spent my days soaking up each bit of sun and smelling freshly cut grass, always wearing bathing suits and barn clothes.

At the age of eight, I welcomed my youngest sister, and our family grew. Our family spent every possible waking moment together. We ate supper together, watched family videos together, sang together, prayed together.

At the age of ten, I began to witness how harsh life could be when it trickled into my family home. I was too naive to understand it, but old enough to feel it. I would say, maybe optimistically, it brought me closer to my sisters. Realistically, it accelerated the end of my blissful childhood. I am just grateful it did not destroy us.

I thank my parents for how they raised me. The discipline. Their blood, their sweat, their tears.

Our conversations always centered around love and gratitude, the blessings we had been given.

At the age of twelve, on one random April day, I was shown one of the world's darker sides. The unforgiving type that tears off a part of you and refuses to give it back.

Our family of six was suddenly five, and I spent endless

Are You Home?

nights dressing myself in my father's clothes, clinging onto the videos of him, relishing every story I heard.

I was scared that I would forget him now that he was gone. I am still scared I will forget him.

The next few years were a blur. I am not sure I could say what exactly happened. All I know is I woke up every day longing to talk to him, to hug him, to say the last few words I never got to say to him. I saw my sisters and my mom, trying to grieve for him—to grieve for us—and who we no longer had: the best man I had ever known, and I was lucky enough to call him dad.

At the age of sixteen, I was preparing to move. Away from my sisters. From my family. From my country. But COVID-19 had engulfed all of us into its terror. I spent the first few months in Barcelona trying to find the light, some kind of hope. That is when I started writing. I had no one else to talk to, so I wrote to my future self. And I thank God that I did.

Eventually, I found that hope, that light, the reason to keep on waking up in the morning. But it did not come easily. That is to say, at times, it still does not come easily. I wish I could cup sixteen-year-old me's face and tell her to keep going.

At the age of eighteen, I am writing this book for me, and for you.

Parados

Event

We regret to inform you that your life has ended as of April 11, 2017.

And your belongings can be found beside your headstone, weeping for the loss.

We are unable to give a reason for the change,
but please trust that we have made the best decision.

Thank you for your service to life.

Are You Home?

Heaven is a cruel place when

you cannot be with the ones you love

when your life ends too early and

there is nothing you can do about it.

I do not want flowers

or condolences.

I do not want to hear stories and

reminisce over pictures.

I just want you.

Only you.

I inhale your cologne,
enveloped in your hug,
whispering, *I love you.*

Our final goodbye.

If I knew it was the last time,
I would have held you longer.

I would have

never

let

go.

What I <u>don't</u> say <u>can't</u> hurt me.

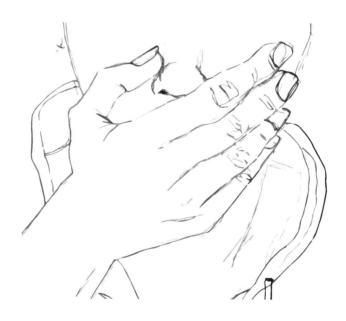

Are You Home?

Episode

Aftermath

No one warned me
how hard it would be without you.

No one told me
of the pain of coming home and
you not being there to hug me.

I miss
seeing you in a crowded room.

I miss
listening to Phil Collins with you.

I miss
the love you gave me and
the best friend I had in you.

Four—now five— years seems like
a little too long without you.

No.

It is too long without you.

I am dreading
having to tell my kids stories about you.

I am dreading
that they will not know you.

Basically, what I am saying is…

I miss
you.

Are You Home?

I do not remember myself before you came into my life.

Was I always this quiet?

Did I laugh at his jokes?

Did I love without worry?

—For: unexpected grief

Your foot is in the door faster than I can close it.

You invite yourself in.

Then leave like nothing happened.

Like being an assaulter is not the same

as being an intruder.

Are You Home?

The hollow hole inside me reopens each time I hear your name.

There is a chasm where my heart should be—and nothing to fill it with.

There is a universe where
I am a book, battered but not broken.

Well loved.

My pages bare my vulnerability. My words are bathed in beauty and in pain.

I do not fear being opened. I do not obscure my meanings.

I am in safe hands. I trust in those who hold me.

I am normally pretty good with directions, but today

I've lost the coordinates for home.

Not all places can be plugged into my GPS.

Not all places can be found.

I do not know who I have become or

        why I am fighting.

If I am the lion,

        who is the lamb?

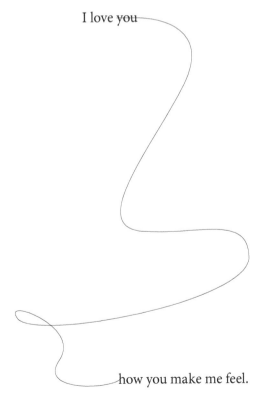

I love ~~you~~

how you make me feel.

My next birthday

I will blow out my last candle…

Wishing to have my face in your hands again.

To have your eyes locked with mine.

To hear the words,

    "You are so beautiful"

        one last time.

      Don't you know why they are called wishes?

          — I am still chasing male affirmation

You are mature for your age.

As if that is a compliment.

You are mature for your age.

As if I was not forced to grow up.

You are mature for your age

As if I was not a product of my trauma.

You are mature for your age

As if it were my choice.

I did everything you said,

I said weeping.

I closed the blinds, locked the door.

I turned off the lights and hid.

Sometimes, my dear,

you said,

The monsters are not out there.

They are in here.

Are You Home?

5 seems like such a

small number, until

I realize. That is how

many years it has been

without you here.

My only hope is that someday,

somebody will make me experience all the emotions

I have forgotten to feel.

Are You Home?

That tingling sensation that travels up my tongue , to my nose, releasing its water in my eyes, happens every time I hear your name.

I used to think I needed the world to be happy.

No, now I realize,

I just needed you.

Are You Home?

I have had to go to sleep 1,918 nights without kissing you goodnight.
Time is NOT healing anything

The world praises
the independent woman until
she rises above men.

Then,
they tear her down
for her success.

What is it with society and irony?

I shouldn't have to earn my place just to be heard.

How do you expect me to look at you and not hate myself?

You have all the things I do not.

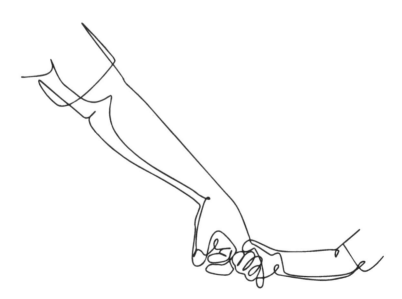

Sometimes
it just does not feel like you were my dad.

Sometimes
I wonder if it is because you knew a different me, loved a different me.

The truth is
you are not here to love this new version of me.

The truth is
my 12-year-old self is still lost without you.

The truth is
my 18-year-old self is still waiting for your love to find me.

I know such a discovery would not fix everything,

I know my problems extend beyond your absence.

I know I would still be broken with you here,

But I would be
        just a little less
                destroyed.

Stasimon

Actualization

I think I am getting stronger…
I have stopped crying on the way back from the airport. I can call
family and not break down. I have started running again. I have started
writing again.

and then I walk into a space where you were or think of a memory that
you held,

and I lose it.

the strength slowly drains out of my body
(almost like the memories, too)

I thought I was doing better,

doing okay.

But growth is not a straight line.

Maybe even here,

I am still growing.

Are You Home?

I am starting to see the beauty in everything.

In people

In change

In love

In loss

In laughing

In crying…

In life.

And it is the most freeing feeling to finally be alive,

To finally welcome every emotion that comes my way with acceptance.

With the understanding that they come and go.

They leave and they return.

And that is okay.

Perhaps that is the beauty of it all.

Maybe it is not the acceptance that is beautiful,
but the heartbreak.

Realizing how much another person can
love you enough to destroy you.

Except, how am I to find the strength to
make amends with the broken pieces
without you here?

You were what I displayed

My broken pride all in one place

My hands still have scars trying to hold you.

You have invited the change in and become it.
Now, I feel lost all over again.

I think I was the liar all along,
Convincing myself I was okay.

This is not another poem about having no hope anymore

No, it is about the light you have given me in every loud laugh that lit up my room.

It is about the car ride to drop you off at the airport, knowing a part of me is leaving here again.

It is about the cruelty of goodbyes and wiping my tears on your college hoodie, smelling your perfume.

I look across the room and I do not see your blonde hair or your green phone case and suddenly I feel empty.

It is your presence that keeps me going, and your absence that leaves me feeling lifeless.

This poem is about the hope you have given me.

And how hard it is to see it fly across the ocean again.

<u>Poetry should be everyone's love language.</u>

When I say I am lost
I mean you are not here.

When I talk about crying at night
I'm saying I cared so much about you.

I love you is written on every page of my notebook,
disguised as I'm sorry.

I WANT TO FEEL
LIKE ME AGAIN

If you find me lying in the sun,

leave me be.

Your warmth has left me so cold.

I am trying to find my way back to my body again.

Are You Home?

In the mornings, when I cannot rise up out of bed,
I think of your strength.
That is enough to pull these weak bones out of
their grave.

—To the woman who raised me

I am beautiful

I am beautiful

I am beautiful

I am beautiful

I am beautiful

Maybe if I say it enough times I will believe it.

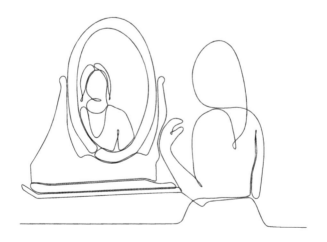

Are You Home?

I inhaled your pain and exhaled my love,

Until I saw my worth.

You were my cigarette.

Writing joy is harder
than writing sadness.

Maybe it makes me a pessimist,
only focusing on the bad,

But maybe it's because we were
told to hide in the dark—

Not to run to the light.

I would say that you ruined me, but that gives you too much power. Instead, I will say that you were the reason my pillow was wet with tears. You gave me love and then took it away—what cruelty. You called me beautiful and then left (and never returned).

You made me hate this body.

I would say you destroyed me, diminished me, hurt me, but believe me, I am not destroyed yet. I am still here standing with both feet on top of your lies. Yes, I had to climb up the mountain of self-love, but the view from here beats anything you ever gave me. It beats everything you ever did.

It takes a lot more than you to destroy me.

Exodus

Beginning

Here I am,

        Stronger than ever,

                More beautiful than ever.

Even though I gave you my time,

I have taken back my joy.

Thank you for teaching me what is worth leaving.

Thank you for showing me what love is not.

Thank you for knowing when to let go

—las manos

My future self is holding me.

Are You Home?

I found redemption in you.

I do not have to be society's daughter.

Social standards
do not dictate
my beauty.

Are You Home?

Air fills my lungs as I prepare for a laugh,
The good type that rises up from the stomach.

I catch myself living in the moment,

And hoping it never ends.

I want so much love that
I cannot help but to share,

Enough pain to draw me
into your arms at night,

And the best kind of fear
For what beautiful beings we will be together.

Are You Home?

I know the weight of the world
rests upon your shoulders.

I see them slowly cave in upon your beautiful body,
encapsulating your generous heart.

And though it is heavy,
It never breaks you.

You are my miracle.

I think of
every freckle
as a place
where an
angel

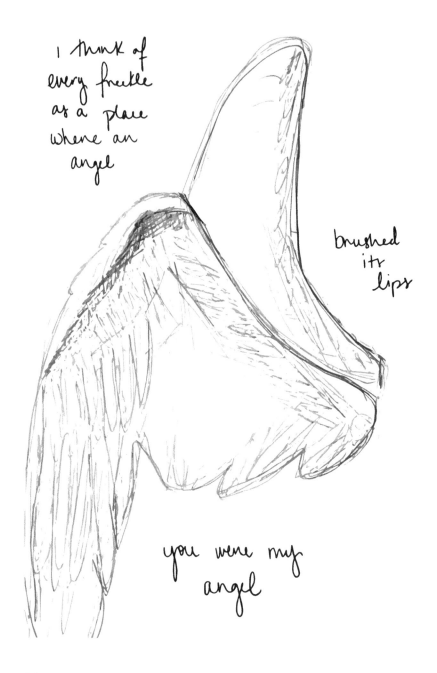

brushed
its
lips

you were my
angel

Are You Home?

You see my brokenness and
you help fix me,
time after time.

Selflessness or magic,
I am not sure which it is.

Maybe they are the same.
Maybe they are not.

But regardless, it is you.

I know who I am is
an ode to who you are.

I am so thankful I am my mother's child.

Slowly, I pull myself back together
from its opposite ends,

Gathering the thousand pieces
of my heart into a heaping pile.

Finally cleaning up my mess—cleaning up myself—
I walk away a stronger person.

Growth comes from destruction.

The best time to leave is before the end credits start rolling. While the theater is still dark so you don't have to wait as those in front of you slowly trickle out. So when you leave, they think you've just gone to the bathroom and you'll be back.

Leaving allows you the freedom of taking matters into your own hands, deciding just how you want this to end.

It gives you power.

But this freedom comes at a price:

Getting less than what you paid for,

Wondering what you missed had you stayed.

When they realize you're gone, they know it was because you were done with them.

They should have held your hand a bit tighter and you a bit longer.

Leaving is an art.

It is spring in the city.

April showers disperse the sorrows of fall and winter.

The purple trees are first to bloom.

They were your favorite.

The birds flock to the warmer weather.

You would harmonize to their melody.

I wear my red zip up again with crop tops underneath.

I am thinking of summer and gelato and staying up till 4 just to sleep in till 3.

How you'd demand for my sleep

even if I could not be more beautiful.

I'm ready for the beach and my olive skin to soak

up the sun another year more.

I think of the waves, and

how they draw me in so strongly or how—

No

—the darkness stays just long enough for me to miss the light.

I am not thinking of you.

Instead, I am thinking of how nice it feels to not have tears on my cheeks,

    to finally be able to laugh

        to trust

           to love myself again.

I have made this city my own.

I wrote my name on its buildings,
Left my tears on its streets,
Slept in its courtyards,
Ran in its gardens,
Sat on its benches in the rain,
Admired its sunsets and glistening lights.

I have met myself again in the process.

I no longer fear loneliness, but welcome it.
I take myself on picnics and dates.
I am careful to love, but do not hold back.
I have embraced my beauty, accepting myself.

I have come home

In that park a few blocks up,
In that cafe on the side street,
At that one road where I can see all the way down to the sea.
In the people that I have met, and have yet to meet.

And it is such a beautiful thing to be here and to be alive.

When I am missing you,

I hold myself a bit longer.

After all, half of me is you.

I wrap myself in memories of you to create a
cocoon in which I fall asleep.

When my memories fail me,

I look at the four strong women around me

Who know more than they say,
smart and beautiful,

Who have achieved more than expected and
kept their soul,

Who give themselves up day after day
for my own sake,

                                                            And I see you.

You would be so proud of the women we are becoming.

I cannot imagine being born into a world without a person
to call my sister.

They are my best friends. I have spent countless nights
sleeping in their rooms, just to be close to them.

I have their numbers saved at the top of my phone,
so when anything happens, they are the first people I tell.
(And trust me, I tell them everything).

They helped do my hair and makeup for my first dance,
helped teach me how to shave my legs. They were the first
ones I ran to when a boy made me cry. They are still the
ones I run to.

My soul has been split into four, each of us carrying a piece
of the other. So, I give thanks to my mother's womb for
carrying all four of us girls. I give thanks for the miracle
of love.

Are You Home?

I will take each bruise,
each torn ligament,
each cracked bone,

I will cradle them in my heart,
as they slowly reform,
knitting back together.

Call me a god
or call it self-love,

Both have the power
to heal the unthinkable.

Do not bother knocking.

I am not here.

I have too much life to live

with such little time.

Are You Home?

Author bio

Isabella Fulbright was born in Florida and lived there until she was sixteen. She started writing about five years ago when her father passed away. Isabella views her work as a reflection of what is inside and uses words to capture those moments. Currently living in Barcelona, she enjoys the city, its culture, and savoring each moment before it ends. Isabella's first collection of poetry and art was published in 2022. As she continues through life, she hopes to connect with, relate to, and inspire those who join her on the journey.

Are You Home?

9 798218 066949